I0901644

WORDS OF WISDOM

A 30-Day Proverbs Journal

Friendship Press®

Copyright © 2023 by Friendship Press

All rights reserved.

No part of this book may be reproduced or utilized in any form or by any means, electronic or mechanical, or by any information storage and retrieval system, without written permission from the publisher.

Friendship Press
P.O. Box 117
Wyncote, PA 19095

Scripture quotations are taken from the New Revised Standard Version Updated Edition. Copyright © 2021 National Council of Churches of Christ in the United States of America. Used by permission. All rights reserved worldwide.

Library of Congress Catalog-in-Publication data available upon request

ISBN (hardcover): 978-1-961088-15-3

Verse selection and prompts by Scott Tunseth
Cover and interior design by Laurie Ingram

Typesetting by Integra Software Services Pvt. Ltd.
Printed in the United States of America

About This Journal

Each *NRSVue Bible Journal* is offered with the hope that you will be inspired by your encounter with scripture and that journaling becomes a helpful part of your devotional journey.

The undated pages allow you to write at your own pace, with scripture passages and thoughtful writing prompts placed at regular intervals for you to meditate on, pray over, and write about as the Spirit moves you.

In this volume, thirty of the most impactful passages from the Book of Proverbs are presented for your reflection. The writing prompts will help you think about how to apply this wisdom in your life today. May the timeless wisdom of Proverbs be a light on your path.

date

PROVERBS 1:7-9

The fear of the LORD is the beginning of knowledge;
 fools despise wisdom and instruction.
Hear, my child, your father's instruction,
 and do not reject your mother's teaching,
for they are a fair garland for your head
 and pendants for your neck.

date

The meaning of "the fear of the Lord*" is closer to respect or reverence than of being afraid. How have you experienced the wisdom of God? Recall a time you learned something important from a parent or other trusted adult. How has this wisdom affected your life or the path you have taken?*

date

PROVERBS 2:6-11

For the LORD gives wisdom;
  from his mouth come knowledge and understanding;
he stores up sound wisdom for the upright;
  he is a shield to those who walk blamelessly,
guarding the paths of justice
  and preserving the way of his faithful ones.
Then you will understand righteousness and justice
  and equity, every good path,
for wisdom will come into your heart,
  and knowledge will be pleasant to your soul;
prudence will watch over you,
  and understanding will guard you.

date

In what ways have you experienced God's wisdom as a shield? Describe how God's wisdom is connected to justice and equity.

date

date

date

PROVERBS 3:3-8

Do not let loyalty and faithfulness forsake you;
bind them around your neck;
write them on the tablet of your heart.
Then you will find favor and high regard
in the sight of God and of people.
Trust in the LORD with all your heart,
and do not rely on your own insight.
In all your ways acknowledge him,
and he will make straight your paths.
Do not be wise in your own eyes;
fear the LORD and turn away from evil.
It will be a healing for your flesh
and a refreshment for your body.

date

How do you, or how would you like to, wear loyalty and faithfulness like a necklace? Create a prayer about this.

Think of a time you relied on your own insight and ignored the wisdom of God or the instructions of someone. What happened? Why is relying on our own insights both dangerous and necessary?

date

date

date

PROVERBS 3:27-30

Do not withhold good from those to whom it is due,
when it is in your power to do it.
Do not say to your neighbor, "Go and come again;
tomorrow I will give it," when you have it with you.
Do not plan harm against your neighbor
who lives trustingly beside you.
Do not quarrel with anyone without cause,
when no harm has been done to you.

date

Think about your neighbors. How would you describe your relationship with them? If you were to give your community a neighborliness score, would it score well? Why or why not?

How about our country? What does a more neighborly world looks like to you?

date

PROVERBS 4:10-14

Hear, my child, and accept my words,
 that the years of your life may be many.
I have taught you the way of wisdom;
 I have led you in the paths of uprightness.
When you walk, your step will not be hampered,
 and if you run, you will not stumble.
Keep hold of instruction; do not let go;
 guard her, for she is your life.
Do not enter the path of the wicked,
 and do not walk in the way of evildoers.

date

For you, what does the "way of wisdom" and "the paths of uprightness" look like. What things keep you from this way or path? What things help you stay on the way or path?

In Proverbs, wisdom or instruction is often personified as being female. Who is the wisest woman you have ever known? What made her so?

date

date

date

PROVERBS 5:15-16, 20-23

Drink water from your own cistern,
flowing water from your own well.
Should your springs be scattered abroad,
streams of water in the streets?

Why should you be intoxicated, my son, by another woman
and embrace the bosom of an adulteress?
For human ways are under the eyes of the LORD,
and he examines all their paths.
The iniquities of the wicked ensnare them,
and they are caught in the coils of their sin.
They die for lack of discipline,
and because of their great folly they are lost.

date

How difficult is it for you to avoid being "intoxicated" by unhelpful thoughts or actions? What disciplines or strategies do you have in your life for avoiding the kind of "follies" that lead to being physically, mentally, or spiritually lost?

date

date

date

PROVERBS 6:16-22

There are six things that the Lord hates,
seven that are an abomination to him:
haughty eyes, a lying tongue,
and hands that shed innocent blood,
a heart that devises wicked plans,
feet that hurry to run to evil,
a lying witness who testifies falsely,
and one who sows discord in a family.

My child, keep your father's commandment,
and do not forsake your mother's teaching.
Bind them upon your heart always;
tie them around your neck.
When you walk, they will lead you;
when you lie down, they will watch over you;
and when you awake, they will talk with you.

date

Have you experienced or been a victim of any of the seven things that the LORD hates? Describe how you felt or how it affected you.

date

PROVERBS 8:10-14

Take my instruction instead of silver
   and knowledge rather than choice gold,
for wisdom is better than jewels,
   and all that you may desire cannot compare with her.
I, wisdom, live with prudence,
   and I attain knowledge and discretion.
The fear of the Lord is hatred of evil.
Pride and arrogance and the way of evil
   and perverted speech I hate.
I have good advice and sound wisdom;
   I have insight; I have strength.

date

In what way is wisdom better than jewels or gold? Why is the contrast often drawn between seeking wisdom and seeking material wealth? What is your view on use of material wealth?

What key insight has emerged for you in the reading of Proverbs so far? How does it give you strength?

date

date

date

PROVERBS 8:22-24, 29-31

"The Lord created me at the beginning of his work,
the first of his acts of long ago.
Ages ago I was set up,
at the first, before the beginning of the earth.
When there were no depths I was brought forth,
when there were no springs abounding with water.

. . . when he assigned to the sea its limit,
so that the waters might not transgress his command,
when he marked out the foundations of the earth,
then I was beside him, like a master worker,
and I was daily his delight,
playing before him always,
playing in his inhabited world
and delighting in the human race.

date

The author of Proverbs says Wisdom was present with God when God created the world, playfully working beside God and delighting in the human race. What creative wisdom does the world and humanity need most right now? What is needed to unleash that wisdom?

date

date

date

PROVERBS 9:1-6

Wisdom has built her house;
  she has hewn her seven pillars.
She has slaughtered her animals; she has mixed her wine;
  she has also set her table.
She has sent out her female servants; she calls
  from the highest places in the town,
"You who are simple, turn in here!"
  To those without sense she says,
"Come, eat of my bread
  and drink of the wine I have mixed.
Lay aside immaturity and live,
  and walk in the way of insight."

date

If you were to build your life on seven pillars of wisdom, what would those seven things be? Why?

date

PROVERBS 10:9-12

Whoever walks in integrity walks securely,
  but whoever follows perverse ways will be found out.
Whoever winks the eye causes trouble,
  but one who rebukes boldly makes peace.
The mouth of the righteous is a fountain of life,
  but the mouth of the wicked conceals violence.
Hatred stirs up strife,
  but love covers all offenses.

date

When you think of a person who has integrity, who comes to mind? Why? Do you walk with integrity? If so, how do you maintain it? If not, how can you get in step with it?

What or who, in your opinion, needs a bold rebuke these days? How can such boldness lead to peace?

date

date

date

PROVERBS 11:12-14

Whoever belittles another lacks sense,
  but an intelligent person remains silent.
A gossip goes about telling secrets,
  but one who is trustworthy in spirit keeps a confidence.
Where there is no guidance, a nation falls,
  but in an abundance of counselors there is safety.

date

Describe a time when words were used to tear you down or to build you up.

Do you need to be more careful with how you speak to or about others? If so, how will you exercise greater care?

date

date

date

PROVERBS 12:15-16

Fools think their own way is right,
   but the wise listen to advice.
Fools show their anger at once,
   but the prudent ignore an insult.

date

Recall a time when you thought you were right but should have listened to wise advice. How did the situation turn out?

How hard or easy is it for you to ignore an insult or a put-down? How can you be more prudent in the face of personal attacks?

date

PROVERBS 13:12

Hope deferred makes the heart sick,
but a desire fulfilled is a tree of life.

date

What hopes do you have that have gone unfulfilled? How are you feeling about this? What desires have been fulfilled? How has this been life-giving?

Write a prayer that addresses your most pressing hopes or desires.

date

date

date

PROVERBS 14:30-31

A tranquil mind gives life to the flesh,
 but jealousy makes the bones rot.
Those who oppress the poor insult their Maker,
 but those who are kind to the needy honor him.

date

Do you desire more tranquility in your life? If so, how will you find it?

How would you describe God's stance toward the poor in these verses? What does this mean for our actions?

date

date

date

PROVERBS 15:23-24, 30

To make an apt answer is a joy to anyone,
  and a word in season, how good it is!
For the wise the path of life leads upward,
  in order to avoid Sheol below.

The light of the eyes rejoices the heart,
  and good news refreshes the body.

date

What "season" are you living in right now? What good word would make that season more fulfilling, or even more joyful?

Consider that path your life is currently on. Do you want to stay that course or find a new path?

date

PROVERBS 16:1-3

The plans of the mind belong to mortals,
 but the answer of the tongue is from the LORD.
All one's ways may be pure in one's own eyes,
 but the LORD weighs the spirit.
Commit your work to the LORD,
 and your plans will be established.

date

What does it mean to commit your plans, your work, and even your talk to God? If this is something you desire, how will it happen?

date

date

date

PROVERBS 17:1, 17

Better is a dry morsel with quiet
  than a house full of feasting with strife.

A friend loves at all times,
  and kinsfolk are born to share adversity.

date

These two brief verses touch on the important relationship most of us share with family or friends. Share some thoughts about the meaning you take from these verses.

Do you have kinsfolk to help you in times of diversity? On whom do you rely most? Why?

date

date

date

PROVERBS 18:4, 7-8

The words of the mouth are deep waters;
 the fountain of wisdom is a gushing stream.

The mouths of fools are their ruin,
 and their lips a snare to themselves.
The words of a whisperer are like delicious morsels;
 they go down into the inner parts of the body.

date

The writer of Proverbs often refers to the power of words to bring life or cause harm. Are you more likely to choose your words wisely to support or guide others? Or do you prefer to whisper bits of juicy gossip? What changes, if any, do you wish to make?

date

PROVERBS 19:6-7, 17

Many seek the favor of the generous,
 and everyone is a friend to a giver of gifts.
If the poor are hated even by their kin,
 how much more are they shunned by their friends!
When they call after them, they are not there.

Whoever is kind to the poor lends to the LORD
 and will be repaid in full.

date

In terms of material wealth, do you consider yourself, rich, poor, or somewhere in the middle? Describe how this affects the way you live your life.

The theme of God's concern for doing justice toward the poor and the outcast appears all throughout the Bible. What acts of kindness have you done, or could you do to help others in need?

date

date

date

PROVERBS 20:5-7

The purposes in the human mind are like deep water,
  but the intelligent will draw them out.
Many proclaim themselves loyal,
  but who can find one worthy of trust?
The righteous walk in integrity—
  happy are the children who follow them!

date

What "deep purposes" do you need to draw out of your personal well of thoughts and intentions? Make a list of them. Why and how are they important for you? How can they change, add to, or reorient your life?

How have you experienced real loyalty? Are you a loyal person? If not, what prevents you from being loyal?

date

date

date

PROVERBS 21:3, 21

To do righteousness and justice
 is more acceptable to the LORD than sacrifice.

Whoever pursues righteousness and kindness
 will find life and honor.

date

How do you define "righteousness" and "justice"? What are the characteristics of each? How are they connected and how are they different?

Can you think of times in your life when you pursued righteousness or kindness? Was it life-giving? If so, how? Did it bring you a sense of honor? If so, how?

date

PROVERBS 22:1-2

A good name is to be chosen rather than great riches,
  and favor is better than silver or gold.
The rich and the poor have this in common:
  the Lord is the maker of them all.

date

Do you agree that having a good name is better than having great riches? If so, why?

How would you like to be remembered by others when you are gone? Try to capture this in a brief epitaph.

date

date

date

PROVERBS 23:4-5

Do not wear yourself out to get rich;
be wise enough to desist.
When your eyes light upon it, it is gone,
for suddenly it takes wings to itself,
flying like an eagle toward heaven.

date

Riches and wealth, in and of themselves, are not evil, so what is the real caution in these verses?

Consider some ways you could have a rich life that are not simply connected to material wealth. How might you pray for such "riches"?

date

date

date

PROVERBS 24:3-4, 13-14

By wisdom a house is built,
  and by understanding it is established;
by knowledge the rooms are filled
  with all precious and pleasant riches.

My child, eat honey, for it is good,
  and the drippings of the honeycomb are sweet to your taste.
Know that wisdom is such to your soul;
  if you find it, you will find a future,
  and your hope will not be cut off.

date

On what foundations has your "house" been built? List some words or phrases. Step back and look at those foundations. Are they the right ones, or do additional supports need to be added? If so, what would they be?

What sort of future do you wish to have? At this moment, what are you hoping for most?

date

PROVERBS 27:1, 19

Do not boast about tomorrow,
  for you do not know what a day may bring.

Just as water reflects the face,
  so one human heart reflects another.

date

How easy or difficult is it for you to live in the moment? Why do you think boasting about tomorrow is discouraged in the first passage? Name what excites you about the near future. What concerns you?

date

date

date

PROVERBS 28:4-6

Those who forsake the law praise the wicked,
 but those who keep the law struggle against them.
The evil do not understand justice,
 but those who seek the LORD understand it completely.
Better to be poor and walk in integrity
 than to be crooked in one's ways even though rich.

date

How can the law or laws be used to assure justice? What injustices do you see around you that need to be addressed? How will you address them?

date

date

date

PROVERBS 29:18

Where there is no prophecy, the people cast off restraint,
but happy are those who keep the law.

date

What prophetic messages do we most need in today's world? Why? If you were called to be a prophetic voice to the world, what would your primary message be?

date

PROVERBS 30:1-4

The words of Agur son of Jakeh. An oracle.
Thus says the man: I am weary, O God;
I am weary, O God, and am wasting away.
Surely I am too stupid to be human;
I do not have human understanding.
I have not learned wisdom,
nor have I knowledge of the holy ones.
Who has ascended to heaven and come down?
Who has gathered the wind in the hollow of the hand?
Who has wrapped up the waters in a garment?
Who has established all the ends of the earth?
What is the person's name?
And what is the name of the person's child?
Surely you know!

date

So many questions! In what ways do you sometimes feel like this person named Agur? What questions make you weary? What do you wish you understood more deeply about God and life?

date

date

date

PROVERBS 30:18-19

Three things are too wonderful for me;
 four I do not understand:
the way of an eagle in the sky,
 the way of a snake on a rock,
the way of a ship on the high seas,
 and the way of a man with a woman.

date

Think about the things in your life and in the world that are wonderful or awesome beyond your full understanding. Make a list of these and spend some time pondering each one.

Create a prayer of thanksgiving and gratitude for the things you listed.

date

date

date